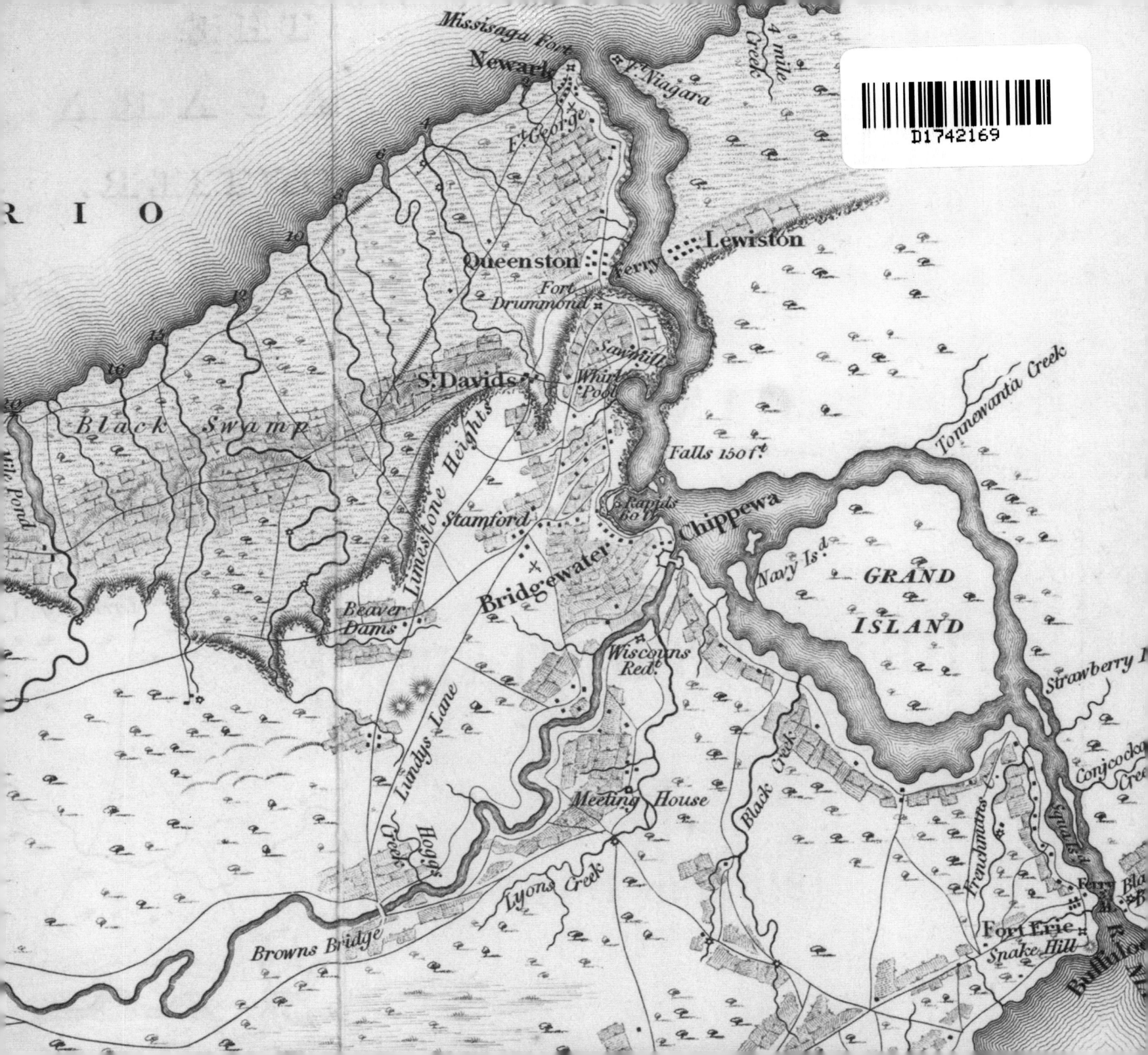

D1742169

NIAGARA
1812 at War

RE-ENACTMENTS ON THE NIAGARA FRONTIER

For Maureen,

All the best, a memento of Niagara

Cosmo Condina

Oct 4, 2016

All rights reserved.

No part of this book may be reproduced or
transmitted in any form or by any means,
electronic or mechanical, including
photocopying, or by any other method
known or yet to be without the prior
written permission of the publisher.
©2012 info@MrBooks.ca

ISBN 978-0-9811415-3-4

PRODUCTION TEAM

publisher | Mr. Books

photography© | Cosmo Condina

research and development | Sheila Kennedy

design | Kennedy Graphics

production coordinator | Mike Burtnik

Digital map reproduction provided by:
Brock University Map Library, War of 1812 digital map exhibit
www.brocku.ca/maplibrary/digital/1812zoom/MAPhome.php

NIAGARA
1812 at War

RE-ENACTMENTS ON THE NIAGARA FRONTIER

PHOTOGRAPHY BY COSMO CONDINA

WITH CONTRIBUTIONS BY

Bob Andrews, Stan Lapinski, Zig Misiak, Matt Straw

SUPPORTED IN PART BY:

www.honhotels.com

PROUDLY PRINTED IN CANADA

THOROLD, ON

ACKNOWLEDGEMENTS

History has a way of repeating itself and chancing upon a War of 1812 re-enactment you would feel transported in time by such an event. It was fate one August weekend in 2007 that I came upon the Siege of Old Fort Erie, an encampment of rows of white canvas tents, filtered with smoke rising through the air from open fire cooking pits and people of all ages dressed in 1812 era clothing.

The evening re-enactment concluded with an atomic blast of gunpowder simulating the explosion of the expense magazine of August 15th, 1814. As the ground shook you could feel the heat of the fireworks, the smell of gunpowder, and see the expression of awe in spectators' faces, it was the real thing!

These 1812 re-enactment events in the Niagara region happen once a month during the summer only, starting with the Battle of Stoney Creek in June, Fort George in July, Fort Erie in August and Fort Niagara in September.

Up until the summer of 2011 I was photographing from the periphery of the action taking place on the field and I was welcomed into the encampments as I got familiar with faces, for they are usually the same ones participating at these events.

My request to be on the field for the Battle of Stoney Creek was approved by Susan Ramsay of Battlefield House through an introduction by Alex Cuberovic a re-enactor friend. It was Alex who made so much of this possible to be accepted and to be made an honorary member of his 104th New Brunswick Regiment, which was to be my home base for future re-enactments. I needed an outfit or a "kit" to blend in and Peter Twist who as the Brigadier General provided an officer's uniform for me.

On the field one experiences an adrenaline rush. Muskets fire, smoke obscures the field, flash in the pan lights faces, regiments move forward, then retreat, warriors howl and scream, soldiers drop to the ground and luckily it is without bloodshed or injuries or death.

All ideas are an abstract thought until acted upon. This book started out as a personal project to create a new portfolio of images and as an exercise to develop a style of photography as I changed over from film to digital capture.

Although a personal project, it gained support as I showed the images and the idea of a book for the bicentennial of the War of 1812 came about. Sheila Kennedy, my publisher picked up on the concept and incorporated historical text by Stan Lapinski. With determination and drive Sheila designed and packaged this project to completion. Also special thanks goes to Bob Andrews for editing and reviewing the historical facts, Peter Martin and Matt Straw for their information on re-enactments, Zig Misiak for a First Nations perspective, Erika Alexander of the Friends of Fort George for support, Parks Canada and the staff of Niagara National Historic Sites for their cooperation with the event/site photography and that of their historic interpreters. The Niagara-on-the-Lake War of 1812 Bicentennial Committee for including me as official photographer of events, and special thanks to all the re-enactors who brave the weekends to make it all happen for the public. Without all this support this project would still only be an idea.

In some ways it was natural that I would take on this project. I was born in Niagara-on-the-Lake and as a child I grew up with Fort George and Fort Mississauga as a background to my fantasies of playing guns with friends. I marveled at the site of Brock's Monument, a column of stone taller than any building in town. Brock must have been a hero for sure I thought. And that foreign land on the other side of the Niagara River was ... *"the enemy!"*

The War of 1812 defined Canada as a nation. We have had a peaceful border for 200 years and Americans cross over to re-enact as friends with friends and not foes. We celebrate a peace on this bicentennial, not a war.

— *Cosmo Condina*

THIS BOOK IS DEDICATED TO

those who devote their time, energy and resources into preserving history for the future.

MAKE READY!

We stand shoulder to shoulder, one hundred wide and two deep in rank and file formation. British Redcoats, Lobsterbacks, the King's soldiers, men of the 41st Regiment of Foot, the 42nd, The Glengarry Light Infantry all. Everywhere around us the smouldering debris of battle lingers. The sour taste and pungent smell of burning black powder invade the mind. As we stand there, muskets loaded, anticipation and adrenaline saturating the double layer wool coats at the height of summer, the smoke finally clears and reveals our enemies fifty yards away. We are given the first of three familiar commands; "MAKE READY!", in unison two hundred muskets are cocked and ready to fire. The second command rings out only a couple of seconds later, "PRESENT!", two hundred muskets lower in unison, poised directly at our common foe. Then, the final command we've been waiting for is finally heard by all. "FIRE!".

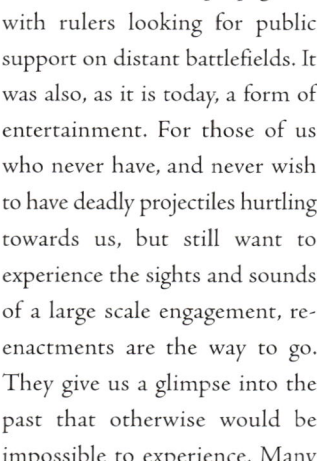

Re-enacting has a long and rich history going back thousands of years. There has always been a need to remember the past and to celebrate it, especially if you belong to the winning side. There are many reasons people choose to be involved in bringing back to life, well, the old ways of life. To those in Niagara this includes not only playing out battles from the war of 1812, but doing the day to day tasks as one may have performed them two hundred years ago. Ask most re-enactors why they dress up in strange costumes and sleep in uncomfortable tents and wear wool coats in the middle of July and most likely you'll just hear, "*Because I love it!*". This may seem unusual to many people but for those involved, it is a labour of love. With an eclectic community of people from all walks of life, featuring a healthy dose of eccentricity, and the great overnight parties of course, it's certainly not hard to believe them.

Re-enactments have been around since the Roman times and were used as a way to display to the public the power and dominance of military leadership. In this sense it became a form of propaganda with rulers looking for public support on distant battlefields. It was also, as it is today, a form of entertainment. For those of us who never have, and never wish to have deadly projectiles hurtling towards us, but still want to experience the sights and sounds of a large scale engagement, re-enactments are the way to go. They give us a glimpse into the past that otherwise would be impossible to experience. Many of the most famous battles we know of, especially during the War of 1812 in Niagara, occurred before the advent of photography, or electronic media. Word travelled by mouth and by letter about what had taken place and artists would literally paint us a picture of what it may have looked like.

In the world of the historical military re-enactment there are several titles given to those who would rather show us what it was like; professional interpreter, historical interpreter, animator and plain old re-enactor. These are the people whose passion and dedication are what bring to life the centuries past. Whether being paid as a student animator at Fort George, Fort York or Fort Erie or one of the many other 1812 era forts across the nation or as part of a volunteer re-enactment group, attention to detail and the pride that goes along with representing those who sacrificed their lives to protect their nation's sovereignty is apparent in the effort put forth.

Every year hundreds of people gather together at local battlefields in period clothing and encampments. As you walk past row upon row of triangular white tents you may notice a surprising amount of men with long sideburns, women wearing dresses and bonnets that combined must total an alarming weight, and cups filled with a suspicious clear liquid, especially in the absence of a water fountain. People are enjoying themselves in an atmosphere found nowhere else but a re-enactment. Circles form around beautiful 18th and 19th century folk music being played with fiddles, spoons and other instruments forgotten to mainstream music such as the bodhrans and dulcimers. People are cooking food over open fire pits, adding ever more variety to the already overwhelmed senses. During all of the hubbub a different kind of music is beginning to play. A lone snare drum begins to beat an order call known as *The Troop* and those with muskets and red coats begin to stand up from their cooking fires and wander over to the assembly area; it's time to go back to the field.

After the enormous crash of sound and stabs of flame erupt all the way down the line of formation it is clear that the enemy is weakened. Our muskets drop to our sides after the command to "ORDER ARMS!". It is time to break our enemy. "FIX BAYONETS!". Now we stand, a hedge of spikes, eighteen inches of cold British steel fixed to the ends our muskets. We have been commanded to shoulder, and port our arms so that our muskets are held in front of us and are angled diagonally up and to the left. This is the final moment before the charge. We begin to march slowly, giving our frightened and demoralized opponents time to consider what awaits them if they remain. As we draw closer, our pace quickens. After what feels like an eternity, we've crossed the field and the time has come. Instinctively our muskets swing down and to the right; our triangular bladed bayonets staring down our enemies. By now we are running as fast as each individual can and at the apex of the charge, right before contact with the defenders the entire line erupts in a unanimous "HUZZAHH!!".

WHY CANADA WAS BRITISH

The Seven Years' War in North America officially ended on February 10, 1763. (The war in Europe was settled five days later by the Treaty of Hubertusburg on February 15.) The British offered France a choice of either its North American possessions east of the Mississippi or the Caribbean islands of Guadeloupe and Martinique, which had been occupied by the British. France chose to cede Canada, and was able to negotiate the retention of Saint Pierre and Miquelon, two small islands in the Gulf of St. Lawrence. France attached comparatively little value to its North American possessions, and French negotiators thought they had made a good deal at the Treaty of Paris. Philosopher Voltaire wrote that Louis XV had only lost *a few acres of snow*. The economic value of the Caribbean islands to France was greater than that of Canada because of their sugar crops. The British, however, were happy to take New France, because they had other sources of sugar.

As a result, because Canada was British, it became a haven for United Empire Loyalists. After the Declaration of Independence in 1776 many Americans who were still loyal to the Crown had their lands confiscated and were being threatened or killed. They took the British offer of free land grants and protection. A large number of these Loyalists settled in the Niagara Peninsula and helped to populate the area with hard-working farmers whose loyalty to Britain helped set this area apart from the new country to the east.

Revolutionary War.

First Nations:
A reference of convenience grouping all First People's Nations and Territories as one. A comparison would be the European Union made up of sovereign nations i.e. France, Poland, Germany.

Western Nations:
A reference of convenience when referring to the many First Nations west of Lake Erie assembled into a confederacy of sorts by Tecumseh.

Six Nations East of the Niagara River:
Composed of twelve separate territories mostly along or near the Niagara River and two others, Onondaga and Oneida, territories around the Finger Lakes further inland.

Wampum:
Two types of shells were used to create the "shell bead" or wampum. Tying several wampum together in specific ways created wampum strings or wampum belts. They were used for similar reasons both carrying the "word" spoken around specific occasions.

Scalp Lock:
The head was shaved leaving a variety of "tails" adorned with turkey feathers, porcupine quills, beads and other items that were personal to the coming of age boys and men.

Turkey Feathers:
Wild turkey feathers were commonly used as the "bird" was respected for its natural attributes such as being stealthy, quick and patient.

FIRST NATIONS

A casual consumer of the history around the War of 1812 might say that the conflict was between Britain and the United States. That belief is not wrong but is incomplete.

The Treaty of Paris in 1783, ended the American Revolution. The fighting between Britain and the fledgling new country was over for them but continued for the First Nations on both sides of the "new" border up to and in through the years of the War of 1812.

Many Western First Nations were rallied by Tecumseh in order to create a strong line of defense against the Americans who were determined to occupy what remained of their traditional lands. They were literally fighting for survival and their very existence.

The Western First Nations sent wampum belts asking for the Haudenosaunee (*Ho-deh-no-shoh-neh*), also known as Six Nations, to support them. The Haudenosaunee north of the Great Lakes needed to protect relations with Britain therefore did not get involved. The Haudenosaunee east of the Niagara were influenced by the Americans and they too stayed away from the conflict in the west.

The declaration of war by the Americans in June 1812 was a short lived blessing for the Western First Nations. More than a military victory the taking of Forts Detroit and Mackinac by the Western First Nations, British regulars, Upper Canada militia and First Nations warriors from the east demonstrated solidarity against a common foe. This victory supported by the British army was absolutely crucial as it secured an exposed western front but more importantly showed the Haudenosaunee, and other First Nations in the east that the British army, though outnumbered, was still a powerful adversary. This victory swayed many warriors in the east to move in support of the British around Fort George and Queenston Heights.

However, on the Niagara Frontier the Haudenosaunee, of the Grand River and those east of the Niagara River were still pulled in two different directions because of conflicting treaty obligations with the British Crown and the Americans. Both the Americans and the British needed their support and every effort was made by each to keep the Haudenosaunee apart, or at the very least neutral, fearing a unified warrior army that would certainly have tipped the scales in favour of whichever side they chose.

The Haudenosaunee of the Grand River and those in Tyendinaga, Kanesatake, Akwesasne, Kahnawa:ke territories had many councils with their relatives east of the Niagara River. They were working out their own strategy for survival. Though geographically separated by great distance they clung to their traditional rules of council and settled on a peace between them. The wampum bound them to an agreement not to fight against one another should they at some point "take up the hatchet" on opposing sides. History taught them many lessons and they were currently living the dismal aftermath of taking sides in wars not of their making.

This "peace between them" remained fragile because the Haudenosaunee of the Grand River made it clear that they were going to engage in battle aligned with Britain and their militia neighbours if the Americans crossed the border into Upper Canada. They had to protect their sovereign territory along the Grand River and the territories of their First Nations cousins in Tyendinaga, Kanesatake, Akwesasne and Kahnawa:ke. They feared that an American victory would be followed by dire consequences.

THE WAR OF 1812

Between 1793 and the summer of 1812, Great Britain had been engaged in two protracted wars with Napoleonic France. The British navy commanded the seas, but to maintain their blockade of French ports, they needed sailors to man their ships and so, for several years before 1812, they impressed sailors they claimed were British deserters. They had been stopping and boarding neutral ships, including those of the United States, on the pretext of checking cargo to determine if it was destined for France.

The Americans objected to the British actions as a violation of their neutrality. Moreover, Britain forced neutral ships with cargo destined for Europe to first stop in Britain and pay duties. France had similar practices, and the United States demanded an end to the harassment of neutral nations by both Britain and France. After years of diplomatic and economic maneuvering – mostly with negative results for the United States – Napoleon conceded. Initially, Great Britain refused to follow suit, and the United States, after debating the matter in Congress for eight months, declared war on Great Britain on June 18, 1812.

James Madison, the United States President, and other American legislators believed that Canada, with a population that included former Americans – the United Empire Loyalists – would be annexed after a show of American force in Canada. It could then be used as a negotiation chip against Great Britain.

When war was declared, the number of British regular troops present in Canada was 6,034, plus Canadian militia. On the other side, the United States regular army consisted of fewer than 12,000 men. Both sides had bands of First Nations allies. The warriors on the British side numbered in the thousands while those on the American side numbered only in the hundreds.

In the summer and fall of 1812, United States forces, under the commands of Brigadier-Generals William Hull, Alexander Smyth and Stephen Van Rensselaer, and Major-General Henry Dearborn, were directed to invade Canada at Detroit, Niagara, and Montreal. However, inadequate preparations, poor leadership, and untrained troops undermined the invasions. First, on August 16, the British, led by Major-General Isaac Brock, together with Tecumseh and Shawnee, Delaware, and other Western Nations, captured Fort Detroit from Brigadier-General William Hull. On October 13, Brock and Major-General Roger Sheaffe defeated the American invaders led by Generals Stephen Van Rensselaer and Alexander Smyth at Queenston Heights. Dearborn's march against Montreal was called off after only one minor engagement in November. American efforts by Major-General William Henry Harrison and Brigadier-General James Winchester to retake Detroit were also unsuccessful; Winchester surrendered his army to British and First Nations forces on the Raisin River in Michigan Territory on January 23, 1813.

It was clear by then that the Canadians would not willingly join the United States.

Although the territorial holdings in the Niagara Peninsula of both Britain and the United States were returned to their original state when the war ended, the involvement of Canadians in this war helped foster a Canadian identity and national pride which eventually led to the formation of a country in 1867.

Historic interpreter wearing a cavalry general's hat and a blue frock coat that was an undress item worn by many officers.

SIR ISAAC BROCK AND
THE BATTLE OF QUEENSTON HEIGHTS

Isaac Brock was born on October 6, 1769, at St. Peter Port on the island of Guernsey.

At the age of 15, he entered the army as an ensign. By 1802, he was a lieutenant-colonel in command of the 49th (Hertfordshire) Regiment of Foot.

In 1802, Brock and his regiment were sent to Canada. He was promoted colonel in 1805. For a year, beginning in September, 1806, he was temporarily in command of the entire British army in Canada. During that time, he strengthened defenses and made plans for a navy, called the Provincial Marine, which proved to be invaluable for transporting the army. In 1807, Brock was appointed brigadier-general. He commanded the garrison at Quebec until 1810, when he took command of all forces in Upper Canada. In June, 1811, he was promoted major-general, and in October, Brock was made Senior Officer Commander of the Troops and the provisional Senior Member of the Council, putting him fully in charge of both the military and civil authority in Upper Canada. Over the opposition of the provincial legislature, Brock used his authority as chief administrator, to strengthen the militia and reinforce defences. He also worked to strengthen alliances with First Nations as he knew their support would be critical for any successful defense of Upper Canada.

When the United States declared war against Britain on June 18, 1812, Canada was in better military shape than it would have been without Brock.

On July 12, an American army under Brigadier-General William Hull invaded Canada at Sandwich – present-day Windsor. Thanks to Hull's over-cautious nature, the invasion was repelled by the newly formed Canadian militia. Hull withdrew to Fort Detroit. On August 8, Brock embarked at Port Dover on Lake Erie to reinforce the British garrison at Amherstburg on the Detroit River, downstream from Fort Detroit. He arrived on August 13, and joined forces with the influential leader of the Western Nations, Tecumseh. Although they were outnumbered by the Americans, they bluffed Hull into thinking that they had more professional troops and First Nations allies than they actually had, and on August 16, Hull surrendered without firing a shot. For this achievement Brock was acclaimed the "hero of Upper Canada" and named a Knight Companion of the Order of the Bath, although news of his knighthood did not reach Canada until after his death.

After his victory at Detroit, Brock took large quantities of the captured weapons and ammunition back to Niagara to reinforce his position there. Understanding the logistics of warfare he knew that if the Niagara River transportation corridor fell that none of the posts to the west could be supported.

With the intention of possessing Upper Canada before the winter set in, the American army decided to take control of the Niagara River by invading at Queenston, south of Fort George. The Battle of Queenston Heights was the first major clash of arms in the War of 1812.

At 4:00 A.M. on October 13, 1812 an American force left Lewiston on the east side of the river for Queenston 200 metres away on the west side, and a little more than twelve hours later on the same day it was over, with the surrender or capture of 955 Americans.

In between, the battle ebbed back and forth with first one side having the advantage and then the other.

The Americans, under the command of Major General Stephen Van Rensselaer, attacked in 13 boats, three of which were swept down

Niagara River between Queenston and Lewiston

stream. Most of the boats carried 30 men, but two could carry 80 men plus field guns or wagons. Ten minutes after leaving Lewiston, the first American soldiers landed at Queenston and they soon came under fire. British guns also began firing towards the landing stage at Lewiston. The American guns returned fire on Queenston.

As light grew, the British artillery became more accurate, and half of the second wave of six American boats turned back to Lewiston, another was sunk and the soldiers in two others surrendered when they landed.

On the morning of October 13 Major General Isaac Brock heard the distant artillery fire but was unsure if the invasion was going to be at Queenston or if that was a diversion from the real attack at Fort George. He directed a few companies of regular troops and a portion of the several hundred First Nations encamped at the Indian Council House to follow him and rushed to Queenston with only a few aides in tow.

For the first hour and a half of the attack, the Americans were pinned down by a redan battery with an 18-pounder cannon and a howitzer. Captain John Wool was ordered to take the redan from above. The redan was lightly guarded and the Americans easily captured it forcing the artillerymen and Brock's party to retreat to the village. Brock sent a message to Major General Roger Sheaffe at Fort George, ordering him to bring as many troops as possible to Queenston. He then resolved to recapture the redan immediately rather than wait for reinforcements. The assault faced heavy fire and Brock was struck in the wrist of his sword arm by a musket ball but soldiered on. His senior officer's uniform plus his tall figure and energetic gestures made him a conspicuous target. He was shot down by an American at a range of barely fifty metres. Brock was struck in the chest, and died almost instantly. The small British force was greatly outnumbered and failed to retake the redan.

With the big British gun no longer a threat, the Americans brought several hundred more soldiers over the river.

Warriors manoeuvered up and around to the cliff of the river. The cover of the woods on the right flank of the American force moving westward was enough camouflage to pin down any advancement until reinforcements arrived.

When the American pickets heard the war cries and began to be assaulted by the warriors on the Heights, spirits on both sides of the river sagged. Those on the Queenston side tried to get back to Lewiston, and those in Lewiston, including the boatmen, refused orders to go back across to get them.

By early afternoon, Brock's replacement, General Roger Hale Sheaffe led a well-planned attack of a large force on the Americans on the Heights. The Americans retreated to the river where there were no boats to evacuate them, and subsequently over 800 surrendered. The army of Upper Canada had won a significant battle, but lost their beloved commander.

On October 16, a funeral procession for Brock and his aide-de-camp, Lieutenant-Colonel John Macdonell, who was also killed in the battle at Queenston Heights, went from Government House in Niagara to a grave prepared for them inside Fort George. British soldiers, Canadian militia and many First Nations people lined the route. The two fallen officers were buried in a bastion of the Fort overlooking the mouth of the Niagara River. The British fired the appropriate salutes which were respectfully returned by the U.S. garrison at Fort Niagara and a temporary ceasefire was agreed to.

A small cairn at the foot of the Niagara Escarpment marks the spot where Brock fell. In 1824, Brock's and Macdonell's remains were moved into Brock's Monument, which overlooked Queenston Heights. That original monument was bombed and heavily damaged in 1840. It was replaced by a larger, more stately structure 56 metres high, which still stands. Brock's remains were buried inside the new monument on October 13, 1853, the anniversary of his death.

An inscription on the monument reads: Upper Canada has dedicated this monument to the memory of the late Major-General Isaac Brock, K.B. provisional lieutenant-governor and commander of the forces in the province whose remains are deposited in the vault beneath. Opposing the invading enemy he fell in action near these heights on 13 October 1812, in the forty-third year of his age. Revered and lamented by the people whom he governed and deplored by the sovereign to whose services his life had been devoted.

Originally buried at Fort George and moved to the site of the first monument in 1824, Brock and Macdonell's remains were moved to the Hamilton family cemetery in Queenston after the memorial structure was severely damaged by an American act of terrorism. They were reinterred under the second monument in 1853.

This hat was ordered from England by Sir Isaac Brock and arrived after his death at the battle of Queenston Heights. It is a black beaver felt hat with an ostrich feather, brass braids and bullion at its peaks. It also has a linen band trim, a black cockade and a double brass coin chain that run to buttons on the top and bottom. The hat is a regulation issue of 1812 for General staff officers of his Majesty's army. It is permanently on display at the Niagara Historical Society Museum in Niagara-on-the-Lake.

THE BATTLE FOR FORT GEORGE

The Battle of Fort George took place from May 25 to 27, 1813.

The American force, under the command of Major-General Henry Dearborn planned and executed a coordinated land and naval attack. Colonel Winfield Scott led the land attack. He had been captured at the Battle of Queenston Heights the previous December and subsequently exchanged. The naval forces were under the command of Lieutenant Oliver Hazard Perry of the United States Navy.

On May 25, the Americans began to bombard Fort George from their positions along the river. The American gunners in Fort Niagara and the nearby batteries used cannonballs which had been heated until they were red-hot, then quickly loaded into cannons and fired. Some log buildings within Fort George caught fire, and the women and children in the fort were forced to take shelter in the bastions.

The commander of the British forces on the Niagara Peninsula was Brigadier-General John Vincent. He knew the attack was coming, but he did not know where the landing would be. He assumed that the Americans would land in front of Fort George on the Niagara River, and so he placed his largest detachment there. He placed a smaller detachment to the west and another that prepared to march to Queenston if necessary.

However, just after dawn on May 27, the first of four American waves landed on the shore of Lake Ontario, just west of the mouth of the Niagara River, under the protective fire of American

schooners. The British defenders were outnumbered as the second and third waves of Americans landed, and Vincent realized that he was in danger of being outflanked and surrounded in the smoldering ruins of Fort George and that the American artillery could bombard the fort into submission. He ordered a retreat south to Queenston. The retreat was so hasty and Scott pursued so closely that the main powder magazine was left by the retreating British. It remains intact to this day.

Two companies of Americans were sent to pursue the retreating British, and guns from the American side of the river continued to bombard them, but the pursuers were delayed by fire from a British battery and while they reorganized, orders were received to break off the pursuit.

Thanks to excellent planning and leadership, the Americans had captured a strongly fortified position with fewer losses than the British.

Vincent continued his retreat to Beaver Dams, near present-day Thorold, where he was joined by other British regular detachments who had abandoned Fort Erie and other posts in the Niagara Peninsula. He temporarily disbanded the Canadian militia, then moved his force to Burlington Heights near the western end of Lake Ontario.

Less than two weeks later, they would again engage the Americans at the Battle of Stoney Creek.

Fort George

In 1796, the British relinquished control of Fort Niagara in compliance with Jay's Treaty which gave the United States effective control of the mouth of the Niagara River and overlooked the British Navy Hall complex on the opposite shore.

Control of the river supply route was essential to the survival of the forts west of the Niagara region so the British set to work immediately to construct Fort George on the heights above Navy Hall at a higher elevation than the old French Fort.

By 1802, Fort George had been completed and became headquarters for the British army, local militia and the Indian Department.

The new fort was a substantial installation, boasting six earthen and log bastions linked by a wooden palisade and surrounded by a dry ditch. Inside the walls, the Royal Engineers constructed a guardhouse, log blockhouses, a hospital, kitchens, workshops, barracks, an officers' quarters, and a stone powder magazine. The superbly designed magazine is one of the few buildings in the town to survive the war.

During the War of 1812, Fort George served as the headquarters for the Centre Division of the British Army. These forces included British regulars, local militia, Haudenosaunee/Six Nations warriors, and Runchey's corps of freed slaves. General Brock and his aide-de-camp John Macdonell were initially buried within the fort after their deaths at the Battle of Queenston Heights.

In May of 1813, Fort George was destroyed by American artillery fire from Fort Niagara and the American shore of the Niagara River. After a seven month occupation by the Americans, the fort was retaken in December following the burning of Newark. It remained in British hands for the remainder of the war. However, it was decided the exposed position, while necessary, would no longer be the key fortification. After the war, the fort was partially rebuilt, and by the 1820's it was falling into ruins. It was finally abandoned in favour of a more strategic installation at Fort Mississauga and a more protected one at Butler's Barracks.

The site was used over the years for agriculture, as part of a golf course and by the Canadian Military as a hospital for Camp Niagara. During the 1930's, the original plans of the Royal Engineers guided the reconstruction of Fort George as a National Historic Site.

Fort George was opened to the public as a National Historic Site in the 1940's and has featured a costumed animation program focused on the War of 1812 for the past 35 years.

Fife & drummers at Fort George.

The "Coloured Corps"

The British military did not normally segregate their soldiers based on ethnicity. Men of African descent served in various capacities in many regiments throughout the Empire. Prior to the War of 1812, Richard Pierpoint, a black loyalist and veteran of Butler's Rangers proposed the formation of a "Corps of Men of Colour" as part of the Incorporated Militia of Upper Canada. Never numbering more than company strength the "Coloured Corps" fought at the Battle of Queenston Heights and Fort George and in 1814 were instrumental in the early construction of Fort Mississauga.

The decision for men of African descent to fight during the War of 1812 was a difficult one as they understood that if captured by the Americans they would not be treated as prisoners of war but would instead be sold into slavery even if they had always been free men.

The Glengarry Light Infantry was similar to that of the 95th Rifles, with the men wearing dark green uniforms with black collars and cuffs.

37

Officers' Quarters

During the War of 1812 the Officers' Quarters building served as the primary accommodation for junior officers and the mess function was part of the Navy Hall complex. Today the facility houses many of the original artifacts connected to the site and is a key element in understanding many of the social and economic realities of the early 19th century. Even an original portrait of Queen Charlotte (the wife of King George III) graces the sitting room.

Fine wine, elegant music and luxurious food stuffs were common prior to the War and continue to have a place in the Officers' Quarters today as this large central building is a focal point for interpretive programming. Discussions with the military surgeon, an impromptu concert on the piano-forte or investigating the remains of a dinner party gone wrong are all available to today's visitors.

During re-enactments the Officers' Mess is a focal point for planning meetings during the day and social activities in the evening.

Historic interpreter
as a surgeon
of the 41st Regiment
at Fort George.

THE BATTLE OF STONEY CREEK

The Battle of Stoney Creek lasted less than forty-five minutes on the morning of June 6, 1813. However, in the predawn darkness, friends were mistaken for foes and killed, and American leaders were captured, wounded or killed, rendering their troops leaderless and aimless.

After the American victory at the Battle of Fort George on May 27, the British commander, Brigadier-General John Vincent, gathered all his troops from the outposts along the Niagara River, disbanded the Canadian militia contingents in his force and retreated with about 1,600 men to Burlington Heights at the west end of Burlington Bay. The Americans were slow to pursue. A brigade under Brigadier-General William H. Winder followed Vincent at first, but he overestimated the size of the British force and opted to wait for reinforcements at Forty Mile Creek – present-day Grimsby. When Brigadier-General John Chandler arrived with a second brigade, he assumed command of the combined force of 3,400. They camped at Stoney Creek on June 5.

British intelligence reported that the American forces were scattered widely and the troops and artillery poorly guarded. As a result, Lieutenant-Colonel John Harvey recommended a night attack. Furthermore, the British received the password of the day from Billy Green, "Wil-Hen-Har" an abbreviation of American Major-General William Henry Harrison's name. The nineteen-year-old also knew the terrain and the positions of the Americans, so he acted as a guide.

At 11:30 P.M. on June 5, Harvey began moving the British force from Burlington Heights, where Dundurn Castle is now located, towards Stoney Creek, a distance of about 11 km. Marching silently, under cover of darkness they advanced undetected on the American positions. One sentry post was taken silently, but at another post a sentry let out a cry of warning. At this, a group of British let out a cheer and the soldiers joined in. As a result, the British position was revealed to the Americans and the element of surprise was lost.

The Americans rallied. They held the high ground and were able to pour both musket and artillery fire into the exposed British line which began to break apart. Despite repeated charges by the British, the American line held, and with the intense fire that the British line was taking, it was only a matter of time before they would have to retreat.

However, things began to go wrong for the Americans. In the heat of the battle, orders were given to move troops and the American artillery was left unprotected. A small group of British volunteers charged the battery just as the Americans were given orders to cease fire. The field guns were captured and the gunners killed. Then, in the darkness, the smoke and the confusion of the battlefield, two American brigadier-generals were captured when they mistakenly took the British for their own men. In addition, one major, three captains and a lieutenant were captured. When the American cavalry charged, they fired on their own men. In all this chaos, the Americans fell back, thinking that they had lost the battle. When day broke, the British hid under cover so as not to show how small a force they were. The Americans returned to their camp and burned their provisions and tents and retreated toward Forty Mile Creek.

Reinforcements were waiting for the Americans at Forty Mile Creek with orders to attack the British. However, a British fleet appeared on Lake Ontario and the American fleet sailed to its home base at Sackets Harbor, New York, under the mistaken impression that the base had been destroyed by the British. With a line of communications that was 64 km long, and no naval support, the Americans decided to return to Fort George. They were actively pursued by the British, and the Americans suffered more casualties and had more men captured before they reached the safety of the fort on June 10. The Americans never again ventured so far into Canadian territory, and the following December, they abandoned Fort George and retreated back across the Niagara River.

THE BATTLE OF BEAVER DAMS

After the American defeat at Stoney Creek and their subsequent retreat back to Fort George, the British deployed detachments of regulars, militia and First Nations allies in a strategy of harassment in order to prevent the Americans from exploiting the foothold they had gained in the occupation of Niagara. One such outpost and supply depot was established at DeCou House* near the Beaver Dam – present-day Thorold – under the command of Lieutenant James FitzGibbon of the 49th Regiment.

On June 24th, 1813 a column of approximately 800 U.S. troops, including cavalry and field artillery, marched towards Beaver Dams in order to surprise and eliminate that outpost. Fortunately for the British, significant numbers of First Nations warriors were arriving in the area from both the Northwest and the Montreal regions. The movement of the American troops was discovered and an ambush was set by approximately 450 First Nations warriors working with a few Indian Department Officers. The ambush was sudden and effective but the Americans feared that if they capitulated a massacre may ensue, so they refused to do so at first. After two to three hours FitzGibbon finally arrived and the American commander Lieutenant-Colonel Charles G. Boerstler surrendered 600 men and both artillery pieces. After the battle it was stated that *"it was fought by the Indians alone, not a single cartridge being expended by the regular troops"*.

Beaver Dams was a major First Nations victory which contributed significantly to the Americans' inability to expand upon their occupation of Niagara and reinforced a feeling of terror felt by many American soldiers towards the warriors of the First Nations.

*DeCou House (also spelt DeCow, Du Coo or DeCew) was built by John DeCew, c.1808, in Thorold Township, Upper Canada.

One of Lieutenant James FitzGibbon's stories of Laura Secord.

In 1827, Lieutenant James FitzGibbon, commander of the British outpost at DeCew House wrote:

I do hereby Certify that on the 22d. day of June 1813, Mrs. Secord, Wife of James Secord, Esqr. then of St. David's, came to me at the Beaver Dam after Sun Set, having come from her house at St. David's by a circuitous route a distance of twelve miles, and informed me that her Husband had learnt from an American officer the preceding night that a Detachment from the American Army then in Fort George would be sent out on the following morning (the 23d.) for the purpose of surprising and capturing a Detachment of the 49th Regt. then at Beaver Dam under my Command. In Consequence of this information, I placed the Indians under Norton together with my own Detachment in a Situation to intercept the American Detachment and we occupied it during the night of the 22d. but the Enemy did not come until the morning of the 24th when his Detachment was captured. Colonel Boerstler, their commander, in a conversation with me confirmed fully the information communicated to me by Mrs. Secord and accounted for the attempt not having been made on the 23rd. as at first intended.

[Moir, John S. Laura Secord, in Zaslow (ed), p.313]

FORT NIAGARA

The Burning Of The Towns

The British capture of Fort Niagara occurred on December 19, 1813.

A month earlier, most of the British forces in the Niagara Peninsula were massed at Burlington Heights at the west end of Lake Ontario, and the plan was to move them to Kingston. However, during the first week of December, Lieutenant-General Gordon Drummond took over command. He knew that the Americans had been defeated at Montreal, and that the American army was stranded in winter quarters in upper New York State. Instead of retreating, Drummond ordered the units at Burlington Heights to advance towards the undermanned Fort George.

Brigadier-General George McClure had about 200 men holding Fort George. On December 10, McClure learned of the British advance. He had no hope of receiving reinforcements and decided his position was untenable, so he evacuated his troops across the Niagara River to Fort Niagara.

As the Americans abandoned Fort George, the order was given to burn the nearby village of Newark – present-day Niagara-on-the-Lake – leaving even women and children without shelter or possessions in the middle of winter. These actions were contrary to the plan approved by the United States Secretary of War John Armstrong, which stipulated that the inhabitants were to be given several days' notice if the Americans had to burn the town to prevent British forces from finding cover.

Once the British retook Fort George, Fort Niagara was vulnerable to a British attack. On the night of December 18, a British force of over 500 men under the command of Colonel John Murray, crossed the river about 5 km south of Fort Niagara. Because of the danger of slippery ice, they were under orders to move with unloaded guns in the event one accidently discharged and the advantage of surprise was lost.

In the village of Youngstown, they captured some American pickets and forced one of the captives to reveal the American challenge and password. The British then used that intelligence to gain entry into the fort. In simplest terms, the British knocked on the fort's door, gave the password and were let in.

The only resistance the British met at Fort Niagara occurred inside, but inevitably, it was captured.

Another British force under Major-General Phineas Riall followed Murray's troops across the river. They captured several American outposts and batteries, and in reprisal for the burning of Newark, proceeded to burn almost every village on the American side of the river, including Lewiston and a nearby settlement of the Tuscarora Nation.

Fort Niagara remained in British hands for more than a year, until it was returned to the United States in 1815 as part of the Treaty of Ghent peace settlement.

THE BATTLE OF CHIPPAWA

Fort Erie was taken by the Americans on July 3, 1814, and on July 4, Brigadier-General Winfield Scott began advancing a force of more than 3,600 men north along the portage road which ran alongside the Niagara River towards Chippawa Creek.

Late in the day, the Americans encountered British defences on the north bank of the creek, near the town of Chippawa. After an exchange of artillery fire, the Americans withdrew a few kilometres. Meanwhile, Major-General Jacob Brown took his troops west to move them across Chippawa Creek upstream.

The British force facing Scott was led by Major-General Phineas Riall. His military intelligence was faulty and this caused him to make decisions he might not have made if his information had been more accurate. First, he thought that the army facing him was smaller than it was. He believed that Fort Erie was still holding out, and that the Americans had left a large number of troops behind to continue the siege. Second, he may also have believed that his opponents were poorly-trained militia. The British confusion about the quality of the American force was caused by the American uniforms. While Scott had been training his men in Buffalo, he had been unable to obtain enough regulation blue uniforms for them. The uniforms he requisitioned had been sent to other posts. Another 2,000 uniforms were ordered to be sent to Buffalo, but because there was a shortage of blue cloth, grey jackets were made instead. Riall did not realize that Scott's grey-clad army was healthy, well trained, well disciplined, and lacked the usual number of inefficient officers; it was arguably the best fighting force the Americans had.

Riall's plan was to cross Chippawa Creek and mount an attack to drive the Americans back across the Niagara River and relieve Fort Erie. The battle began early on July 5, with British light infantry, militia, and a large group of mostly Haudenosaunee warriors leading the way across the creek. They began sniping at the American outposts from the woods to the west. The Americans counter-attacked but when they met Riall's advancing regulars they retreated.

The Americans' first success of the day occurred when their artillery destroyed a British ammunition wagon and put most of the British big guns out of action. Meanwhile, the Americans formed a long line from the woods on the west to the portage road on the east. At first, Riall thought that the American line was composed of grey-clad militia troops. He expected them to scatter after the first volleys, but he realized his error when the American line continued to hold steady under British fire.

Because Riall had formed the British infantry into a line formation to advance over uneven ground with some very long grass, instead of keeping them in a column formation, they advanced awkwardly and became disorganized. Advancing in a line meant that the British moved slowly and had to endure fire from the American artillery for longer. Moreover, instead of taking advantage of the increased fire power which the line formation provided, Riall ordered his infantry to fire only one volley before advancing with the bayonet. Furthermore, as the British moved forward, their artillery had to stop firing to avoid hitting them. Meanwhile, the American gunners were taking a toll on the British. Once the opposing lines were less than 100 metres apart, Scott advanced his wings, forming his brigade into a "U" shape which allowed the flanking units to catch the advancing British troops in a crossfire.

The lines stood less than 75 paces apart and fired repeated volleys. After 25 minutes of this pounding, Riall, who had been wounded by a bullet, ordered a withdrawal. The Americans, with the exception of some Iroquois, did not pursue them. The Americans had won.

On July 7, Major-General Jacob Brown accomplished his original objective and crossed Chippawa Creek upstream of the British defences, forcing them to retreat to Fort George. Because the American navy could not bring him reinforcements or siege artillery, Brown did not attack the fort.

For two weeks the Americans were harassed by Canadian militia and First Nations warriors, but on July 25, the two sides met at the Battle of Lundy's Lane.

THE BATTLE OF LUNDY'S LANE

The Battle of Lundy's Lane took place on July 25, 1814. There were heavy casualties on both sides, caused in part by poorly thought out orders, countermanded orders, poor military intelligence, darkness, and what is euphemistically called today, friendly fire.

After the American victory at the Battle of Chippawa on July 5, an American force under Major-General Jacob Brown pushed the British, led by Major-General Phineas Riall back to Fort George near the north end of the Niagara River. Because the British controlled Lake Ontario, the American navy was unable to transport the men and equipment Brown needed to lay siege to Fort George, and rather than face the British, whose ranks had increased thanks to reinforcements from York – present-day Toronto – Brown moved his men to Queenston a few kilometres south of Fort George. On July 24, after two weeks of being harassed by Canadian militia and Six Nations warriors, Brown moved his troops further south to the Chippawa Creek to replenish his supplies in preparation for a march to Burlington Heights at the west end of Lake Ontario. As soon as the Americans left Queenston, Riall followed with some British soldiers and militia to Lundy's Lane, a side road off the main portage road along the Niagara River 6.4 km north of the Chippawa Creek.

On July 25, Lieutenant-General Gordon Drummond, a man with a lot more experience in administration than on the battlefield,

arrived at Fort George to take command of the British army in the Niagara Peninsula. He immediately ordered a force under Lieutenant-Colonel John Tucker to advance south from Fort Niagara on the east side of the Niagara River, as a ploy to get Brown to evacuate the west bank. Brown's response was to order his men north, with the purpose of getting the British to recall Tucker's troops to protect Fort George. Brown did not know that Riall's force was in Lundy's Lane.

When Riall learned of the American advance, he decided to fall back to Fort George and ordered Colonel Hercules Scott to move his soldiers from St. Davids to Queenston to cover his withdrawal, rather than join him to face the Americans. However, Riall's orders were counter-manded by Drummond, who had force-marched a detachment of reinforcements to Lundy's Lane from Fort George. Therefore, when the first Americans reached Lundy's Lane at about 6:00 P.M., they were surprised to meet a large British force.

The big advantage of the British position was its elevation. The British artillery was massed in a cemetery at the highest point of the battlefield – about 7.5 metres higher than the surrounding ground – and as a result had a good view of the area. This battery became the focus of much of the fighting that night.

American Brigadier-General Winfield Scott's force were first on the scene and suffered the first casualties. In an open field they were easy targets for the British artillery. Scott sent Major Thomas Jesup and his infantry to outflank the British left. They used a path to the river to skirt around the British flank and surprised the British and Canadian units there and drove them back. The Americans now had the portage road and soon they had the junction of the road and Lundy's Lane. Around this time, Riall, who had been wounded, and militia cavalry leader Captain William Hamilton Merritt, among others, were taken prisoners.

In the face of American resistance and Jesup's outflanking maneuver, Drummond decided to pull back, but that had the consequence of leaving the British artillery unprotected.

As night fell, Brown arrived from Chippawa with the main American force and one of his first orders was to send Lieutenant-Colonel James Miller to capture the British guns.

While the British were distracted by another attack, Miller's troops got close enough to the British artillery to fire a volley of musketry which killed most of the gunners. The Americans followed up with a bayonet charge which captured the guns and drove the British from the hill. The British infantry immediately behind the guns tried to counter-attack, but were driven back by the Americans who now held the high ground.

Meanwhile, the British troops from St. Davids under Colonel Hercules Scott arrived on the field. Unaware of the situation, they blundered into an American brigade and were driven back, losing their artillery in the process.

While the Americans tried to set up their own artillery among the captured British guns on the high ground, Drummond reorganized his troops and mounted an attempt to retake his own cannon. The attack was beaten back after a short-range musketry skirmish in which both sides suffered heavy casualties.

In the confusion of the battlefield and the darkness, the Glengarry Light Infantry, dressed in green, were mistaken for Americans by other British units and forced to withdraw after suffering casualties from British fire.

Undeterred by his first failure, Drummond launched a second assault to retake the British artillery. Again the American units stood their ground. While the combat was taking place, Winfield Scott led his men in an unauthorized attack against Drummond's line. Again darkness and battlefield confusion contributed to the havoc, as Scott's men were fired on by both the British and Americans. Drummond's line was driven back but Scott's men retreated.

Shortly before midnight, Drummond launched a third attack to recapture the artillery. By this time the British line consisted of men from remnants of a number of different units. The fighting over the artillery was even closer than before, with bayonets being used at one point, but again the exhausted British fell back.

By midnight, six hours after the battle began, both sides were spent. Only 700 Americans were still standing in the line, and Winfield Scott and Jacob Brown were both wounded. Brown ordered a retreat. The British still had 1,400 men on the field but they were in no condition to interfere with the American withdrawal. Drummond, who was also wounded, ordered some units to hold the portage road and left some light infantry outposts near the Americans, but withdrew the rest a short distance along Lundy's Lane.

At daybreak on July 26, Brigadier-General Eleazer Wheelock Ripley returned to the battlefield to recover the abandoned British guns. He arrived with 1,200 soldiers, including reinforcements from Chippawa, but found Drummond facing him with 2,200 men. Ripley opted for discretion, and fell back.

The American army retreated to Fort Erie, and the British withdrew to Queenston and did not pursue the Americans. As a result, the Americans had time to reorganize and to prepare Fort Erie for defence.

FORT ERIE

Americans Capture Fort Erie – July 3, 1814

British Fort Erie was located at the southern end of the Niagara River near its source at Lake Erie. In 1814, it was the site of several battles between the British and American forces.

The fight over the fort began in 1812, when two American attempts to take it failed.

In May 1813, after the Americans captured Fort George, the British withdrew all their forces from the Niagara Peninsula and retreated to Burlington Heights at the west end of Lake Ontario. The Americans then occupied the abandoned Fort Erie. Later in 1813, the Americans moved a large number of troops from the Niagara area to northeast New York State to attack Montreal. In December, the British took advantage of the reduced number of American troops in Niagara and retook Fort George, then captured Fort Niagara and retook Fort Erie.

For 1814, the Americans planned another invasion of Upper Canada, under the command of Major-General Jacob Brown. Because British ships controlled Lake Ontario and British soldiers held both Fort George and Fort Niagara, the focus of the American attack was the southern Niagara Peninsula.

Since the American troops were already stationed at Buffalo and Black Rock, New York, across the Niagara River from Fort Erie, the

attack was launched from there.

On July 3, Brigadier-General Winfield Scott crossed the Niagara River in the dark and landed 3 km north of Fort Erie. Brigadier-General Eleazar Wheelock Ripley led his forces across the river to the south of the fort. As the American forces approached Fort Erie, the greatly outnumbered British put up a token resistance, then surrendered.

The Siege and Final Assault : August 2 – November 5, 1814

In the three weeks after capturing Fort Erie, on July 3, 1814, the Americans had made improvements to it. Most significantly, since the fort was too small to hold the entire American force, they had extended the earth wall which protected the east-facing front of the fort to the south for an additional 800 metres to a sandy rise known as Snake Hill, where they constructed a gun battery. To protect the fort's north side, the Americans put up another earth wall connecting the fort's northeast bastion to the lake where there was another fortified gun emplacement.

The British, under Lieutenant-General Gordon Drummond, were slow to pursue them after the Battle of Lundy's Lane giving the Americans an additional week to reorganize before the siege.

Shortly after arriving at Fort Erie on August 2, a British force led by Lieutenant-Colonel Cecil Bisshopp was sent across the Niagara River to raid Buffalo and Black Rock hoping to capture or destroy American supplies and provisions. The raid was a failure.

The next British action was more successful. While the British constructed their siege lines and batteries, three American schooners, the Ohio, Somers and Porcupine, anchored in the river, hampered their work by harassing them with gunfire. On the night of August 12, the British launched a boarding attack on the American ships in six boats which had been moved overland from the Niagara River below Niagara Falls. The British captured the Ohio and Somers, but the Porcupine escaped.

This success was followed by failure. On August 13, the British artillery opened fire on the fort, however, the British guns were too far away and the bombardment was ineffective.

The main attack took place after sunset on August 15, in pouring rain. Drummond launched a three-pronged offensive; one against the Snake Hill defences at the south, one against the north batteries, and one towards the fort proper.

The assault on Snake Hill did not go well. The ragtag British force led by Lieutenant-Colonel Victor Fischer, was composed in part of units which had suffered casualties in previous engagements, and former prisoners and deserters from the European campaign. These Europeans were not trusted to the point that they were ordered to remove the flints from their guns and attack with their bayonets. Surprise was lost when an American picket heard the British and fired a shot to alert the defenders. After several attempts to storm the battery in the face of heavy fire, many British fled, and in so doing, created havoc among the soldiers to their rear who were standing firm. Those who did try to scale the defences found that some of the siege ladders built for the attack had been made without taking the depth of the ditches into consideration and were too short to get over the wall. One British company attempted to get around the American defences by swimming in the river. However, the current was too swift, and some of the men drowned. Those who survived were captured. After several unsuccessful assaults, the British decided that another attempt would be futile and they retired.

The attack on the north end of the fort went even worse. It was launched as soon as shots were heard from Snake Hill. Again surprise was lost when American pickets detected the British and fired muskets to alert the defenders. Once the British had moved close enough, the guns of the fort and the battery and several hundred American infantry opened fire. The British, who were jammed into a narrow front between the embankment and the lake suffered heavy losses, including the commander of the attack, Colonel Hercules Scott.

The assault on the fort was more of an equal battle. It was led by Lieutenant-Colonel William Drummond, nephew of Lieutenant-General Gordon Drummond and began well for the British. After the attacks on the north and south ends of the fort were in progress, the British used darkness and the heavy smoke that hung over the field as cover. They crept through the defensive ditch and caught the American artillery men of the northeast bastion by surprise. The gunners abandoned their guns and fled. Those who stood and fought were killed. The Americans inside the fort replied by firing a barrage into the bastion, killing William Drummond, among others.

Meanwhile, the British twice charged through a gap 2 metres wide between the fort's two barrack buildings into the parade ground, but were unable to break into the barrack buildings and mess hall. The Americans continued to try to recapture the northeast bastion but were repeatedly driven back. After nearly an hour of unsuccessful attempts, American gunners turned around a cannon on the fort's rear redan and fired into the northeast bastion less than 46 metres away. The British responded by turning one of the captured cannons around and knocking the American cannon off its carriage.

Shortly after the British began firing their captured gun, a large powder magazine below them ignited. The explosion was immense, destroying the entire northeast bastion and most of the attached barracks building, and killing many British and Canadians. The Americans in the fort fared better because they were sheltered from the explosion by the barrack buildings. The surviving British, fearing that the fort was mined, retreated.

The British offensive on August 15 was a failure. However, although they suffered heavy casualties, suffered sickness and had little protection from heavy autumn rain, the British maintained the siege.

Inside the fort, opinions as to what to do varied. Some counseled abandoning the fort. Some counseled waiting out the British, but the only person whose opinion mattered, Major-General Jacob Brown, decided to attack.

On September 4, an American detachment was sent out to assault the British Battery No. 2. After almost six hours of fighting, a severe thunder storm brought hostilities to an end.

On September 15, the British completed the construction of Battery No. 3 at the western end of their siege lines. From this vantage point, the British artillery could fire at most of the American defences. Brown had no option but to capture Battery No. 3, and put the guns out of commission.

They began by clearing a trail through the woods behind the battery. Then, at noon on September 17, an American force, under cover of heavy rain moved along the trail, and surprised the British soldiers who were guarding the end of their siege works, and captured Battery No. 3. Simultaneously, American infantry charged the British centre. Attacked from both front and flank, Battery No. 2 was also captured.

For two hours the battle raged, but the Americans were unable to capture Battery No. 1. They were also driven out of No. 2 and No. 3. In the face of these defeats, the Americans returned to the fort.

Three of the six siege guns in Brown's primary target, Battery No. 3, had been destroyed. However, the Americans had been prevented from disabling the gun before being driven back.

Ironically, because of illness among the men, the incessant rain and lack of proper shelter, Drummond had already decided to lift the siege, and the day before the American counter-attack, September 16, he had given orders for his artillery to be moved to Fort George. Only a shortage of draught animals had delayed his departure. On the night of September 21, the British force withdrew to the Chippawa Creek.

Coincidentally, on that same day, September 21, American Major-General George Izard arrived at Fort Erie with reinforcements. Since Izard was the senior officer, he assumed command from Brown. Although the Americans greatly outnumbered the British, Izard waited until October 13 before he began an advance. The British, having been given a three week respite, had recovered much of their health and morale, and had strongly fortified the line at the Chippawa Creek. After some indecisive exchanges of artillery fire at the mouth of the creek and a minor success against a British outpost at Cook's Mill on October 19, Izard withdrew.

With the British navy in control of Lake Ontario, the American supply lines to the Niagara front were in jeopardy, a situation made more dire by the onset of winter. On the other side, the British were able to reinforce and resupply their troops. Faced with this situation, Izard, who was short of supplies, decided to abandon Fort Erie and spend the winter in the safety of New York State. On November 5, the Americans set mines and demolished the fort before retiring across the Niagara River.

The British never rebuilt Fort Erie.

Siege of Fort Erie

The Siege of Fort Erie has become known as the "Largest Annual Re-enactment in Canada". 2012 marks the 26th anniversary of the event that continues to grow with each passing year. A re-enactment such as "The Siege of Fort" has several stages of planning and development that start years before the event takes place.

People who re-enact military time periods such as the War of 1812 put in an incredible amount of personal time, money and effort to make historic sites come to life. They often aren't paid, travel vast distances and spend an immense amount of time and research making sure that they are respecting the people that they are portraying. They do it because they love it.

Organizers of these events must work closely with the dedicated re-enactors to develop the battle plans, listen to their concerns and consider improvements. This relationship is crucial in delivering a successful re-enactment event that is enjoyable for all as well as the public who come to watch.

As one can imagine there are a lot of logistics that go into putting on a re-enactment. Concerns for both participants and spectators must be taken into account. The volunteers who come to the site have needs that must be met to ensure a comfortable stay. Things like firewood, straw, washroom facilities, drinking water and food are all ordered ahead of time. Safety lines, emergency plans, pyrotechnics, permits and staffing needs are also prepared in advance.

Both organizers and re-enactors put in their time, research and resources to ensure that the visitor will have an authentic historical experience. They love what they do and when asked, one re-enactor said "It started out as a hobby, became a passion and ended up as an obsession."

A group from the 104th New Brunswick Regiment.

THEY STOOD ON GUARD

The War of 1812 was a learning and maturing process for all those involved. Ten armies of the United States undertook invasions of British North America but all were pushed back to their own side of the border without a hectare gained on either side.

At the outbreak of the War many of the senior U.S. military officers were veterans of the American Revolution who, in the 19th century, had been elected or appointed to positions of authority for political reasons. The passing of more than a quarter century since they last saw military action had taken its toll on their confidence and capabilities. They were quick to realize that militia units could be effective for defensive purposes but in order to undertake a successful invasion a professional army was necessary.

The British military of the time was locked in a bitter struggle with Napoleon in Europe and although they could not afford to dedicate many troops to North America the regiments that were in Canada were well trained and professionally lead. Upper Canada became the primary theatre of war but a successful defence would not have been possible without the support of troops, First Nations allies and resources from Lower Canada, Newfoundland, New Brunswick, Nova Scotia, Prince Edward Island and the Northwest. One of the unforeseen benefits of the War of 1812 was that it was the first step toward the union of colonies into what one day would become Canada.

The last battle to be fought in the Niagara Peninsula was at Cook's Mills on Lyon's Creek on October 19, 1814.

On December 24, 1814, the Treaty of Ghent was signed in Europe, ending the war. However, news of the treaty was slow to reach North America, and on January 8, 1815, the last major battle ended with the United States victory at New Orleans. The United States did not ratify the Treaty of Ghent until February 17, 1815.

The First Nations peoples were the clear losers of the war, not for military reasons but for political ones. Article IX of the Treaty of Ghent was supposed to return First Nations territorial and other rights of the pre-war period but it was quickly ignored by the United States and the war weary Great Britain had little desire for the renewal of hostilities in North America over First Nations rights.

FIRST NATIONS

GOLIATH vs. DAVID

It was Goliath versus David. Upper and Lower Canada, as well as First Nations territories were being threatened by occupation and annihilation.

The First Nations and the neighbouring settlers were defending their homeland, their families and their very existence.

The Haudenosaunee (Six Nations), bound by their ancient traditions, held on to the agreement among themselves not to confront one another in battle regardless of their separate settlements and alliances with the British and Americans. Haudenosaunee and other warriors of the First Nations stood next to their British allies in battle at Fort Detroit, Queenston Heights, York, Fort George, Beaver Dams without having to meet their American allied relatives.

All of this changed dramatically in July of 1813. The wampum belts that had been exchanged between the Haudenosaunee, referring to the peace between them, symbolically broke. Warriors allied to the Crown crossed the Niagara River at Fort Erie entering the territory of their relatives in the Buffalo area. Immediately, in response to this aggressive act, the Haudenosaunee on the east side of the Niagara River officially declared war on Britain.

A few months later in September 1813, with the British abandonment of Fort Malden, south of Detroit and the death of Tecumseh the following month, the fate was sealed for the Western Nations Confederacy. Their dream of unity evaporated. An exodus of entire families of First Nations, loyalists, settlers, and British soldiers, fled the area to safety among the allied stronghold in and around Burlington Heights. These warriors joined the Niagara campaign.

The declaration of war by the Haudenosaunee back in July gave warriors on opposing sides the freedom to engage; warriors occasionally met, individually or in groups, killing or wounding one another. The Battle of Chippawa was one of the most significant conflicts of the war for the First Nations especially the Haudenosaunee. It was this battle that was the culmination of their worst collective fears. They killed one another on an unprecedented scale. Their losses and pain echoed into their villages and most certainly saddened the spirits of their ancestors. The darkness of this reality haunts them to this day.

The War of 1812 Bicentennial Commemoration is an opportunity to repair damaged bridges of the past and to collectively build new ones. The strength of these bridges will be determined by the spirit of those willing to work together, with the intention to meet in the middle, and the desire to "polish the Covenant Chain" cooperatively.

The "Covenant Chain" existed within the Haudenosaunee Confederacy before contact and offered to other nations outside the Confederacy. After contact it metaphorically evolved from rope and iron with the Dutch and the French to silver with the British. The principles, however, for each remained constant being "Peace, Friendship and Respect". The "Covenant Chain", during the War of 1812, existed with the British and Americans and continues to exist with Canada. Over time when any one of the three "links" were imposed upon it would become dull, begin to tarnish. It is said the chain brightens, by symbolically polishing it, when the terms of the covenant are being renewed and strengthened.

... as long as the sun shines upon the earth;

as long as the waters flow;

as long as the grass grows green, peace will last.

Fort Mississauga, Niagara-on-the-Lake, Ontario, Canada

After the reoccupation of Fort George in late 1813 the British decided to construct a new fortification to control the mouth of the Niagara River at Mississauga Point, the location of the first Lighthouse constructed on the Great Lakes. The construction of Fort Mississauga, an irregular star-shaped field work was started in 1814 but was not completed in time to take an active role in the War. While plans were laid in 1816 to have the work replaced by a massive fortress, this was never done as there was little public inclination to undertake that type of huge military expenditure.

Periodically Fort Mississauga was occupied and used throughout the

Fort Niagara, Youngstown, New York, U.S.A.

19th century but was eventually abandoned to the elements. The wooden buildings and picketing are all long gone and the lake has eroded much of the glacis (earthworks) on the northern side. Today the main brick tower of Fort Mississauga has been stabilized and the public is welcome to visit the grounds and take in the spectacular viewscapes of Fort Niagara on the opposite side of the River and the contrasting Toronto skyline on the other side of Lake Ontario.

HISTORICAL RE-ENACTMENTS

The modern day work environment is one dominated by safety and equality. The work environment of the early nineteenth century, especially for a soldier, was one filled with hardships, danger and strict hierarchy. In our attempts to portray these soldiers' lifestyles as accurately as possible, a few exceptions that must be made for personal safety and equality at the cost of complete historical accuracy.

Possibly one of the most visually obvious differences when viewing a battle or the photos taken there are the women standing in line as soldiers. Female re-enactors often have to respond to questions or statements such as, *"There were no women back then!"* Of course what they actually mean to say is that women were not soldiers at the time, which is true.

Today however, people of any race or gender are encouraged to participate in any role within the re-enacting community.

Personal safety is also more important to the community than perfect historical accuracy. This may include minor changes to protocol for reloading weapons (with blanks as opposed to their deadly metal counterparts), aiming muskets at an angle away from your opponents to avoid sending a jet of flame directly at them, and other small modern adjustments to the weapons to protect the user and observer. Things such as non-period eyewear are also accepted, as proper eyesight is often considered important for personal safety at such events.

There are less accepted diversions from historical accuracy that are nevertheless inevitable, mostly in the department of clothing and uniforms. You may catch a glimpse of a modern shoe, cigarette, watch or jewelry. A more difficult problem is the fact that uniforms of the time were very complex. From the exact arrangements of buttons, seams, and various coloured cuffs and collars, to the different variations of each type of uniform that denotes unit and rank these uniforms were often changing. Re-enactors have a limited means of arranging their own personal uniforms to match exactly with one another. While avoided as much as possible, these discrepancies can often remain unrecognized to the untrained eye.

The following pages are photos of re-enactments other than the War of 1812 that are played out in the Niagara area on both sides of the border.

Powder horn cartouche

This structure is the only part of Fort George that survived the War of 1812. It is the oldest military building in Upper Canada.

PLACES TO VISIT AND
OTHER SOURCES OF INFORMATION

FORT GEORGE NATIONAL HISTORIC SITE
www.pc.gc.ca/fortgeorge

FRIENDS OF FORT GEORGE
www.friendsoffortgeorge.ca

FRIENDS OF BATTLEFIELD HOUSE
STONEY CREEK
www.battlefieldhouse.ca

NIAGARA FALLS HISTORY MUSEUM
www.niagarafallshistorymuseum.ca

NIAGARA HISTORICAL SOCIETY MUSEUM
niagarahistorical.museum

OLD FORT ERIE
www.niagaraparks.com/old-fort-erie

OLD FORT NIAGARA
oldfortniagara.org

WOODLAND CULTURAL CENTRE
Brantford, ON
www.woodland-centre.on.ca

COSMO CONDINA

A professional photographer since 1985, Cosmo Condina is known for his subtle, and beautiful travel images. His photographic journeys have taken him across Canada, the USA, Mexico, the Caribbean, Europe and New Zealand.

As an associate photographer with Getty Images since 1990, and also the stock agencies Alamy, SuperStock, Robert Harding and Stock Connection, Cosmo's work is licensed for commercial and editorial use worldwide. Corporations that have used his images for advertising include American Express, Visa, United Airlines, Molson's Brewery, Ontario Savings Bonds and Fuji Film.

A graduate of Niagara College Graphic Arts program in 1976, Cosmo's first book was published in 1984: *Niagara-on-the-Lake A Bicentennial Tribute To The First Capital Of Upper Canada. Niagara At War, 1812: Re-Enactments On The Niagara Frontier* commemorates the bi-centennial of the War of 1812 and is the first of two current projects to be published on the Niagara region. The next volume, *Niagara At Peace* with a foreword written by Christopher Newton, showcases the Niagara area in all its splendor during the four seasons, with spectacular photos of interest to the visitor as well as the local resident.

Cosmo continues to live in Niagara-on-the-Lake, Ontario, Canada where he was born.

www.cosmocondina.com

CONTRIBUTORS

Bob Andrews - *facts and forts*
Niagara-on-the-Lake native and long time employee of Parks Canada, Bob has a background in history and Native Studies and has extensive experience in historic interpretation and public education. Over the years he has been involved in both military and fur trade re-enactments.

Sheila A. Kennedy - *research, development, design*
In addition to the three books mentioned by Stan Lapinski, Sheila designed *Images of a Century, The City of Niagara Falls, Canada 1904-2004*, and two other book design/publish projects with hockey writer John Hewitt, *Garden City Hockey Heroes*, and *The Flyers and The Thunder*.
kennedygraphics@sympatico.ca, sheila@mrbooks.ca

Stan Lapinski - *historical text*
A retired English teacher, Stan taught at Denis Morris High School for 32 years. He has collaborated with Sheila Kennedy on three other books: *Denis Morris High School: A Rowing Tradition Since 1959, The St. Catharines Rowing Club: 100 Years in a Row* and *Brock University Athletics: 40 Exciting Seasons of Generals and Badgers*. He is a volunteer at the St. Catharines Museum and the official photographer for the Canadian Secondary Schools Rowing Association and Royal Canadian Henley Regattas.
www.goldmedalphotos.com

Zig Misiak - *First Nations*
Zig is very clear in stating that he speaks about but not for the Haudenosaunee. In addition to providing curriculum and related support to schools in Ontario and other parts of Canada, Zig's mission is to familiarize, coach, present, and mentor all those interested in Six Nations history and culture seeking a balance between written and oral tradition, while recognizing and respecting the validity of both. Zig is chairman of the War of 1812 Bicentennial Commemoration Steering Committee, Brantford & County, author of *Western Hooves of Thunder, War of 1812*, and historical re-enactor, Butler's Rangers American Revolution and Caldwell's Rangers War of 1812. www.realpeopleshistory.com

Matthew T. Straw - *foreword, re-enactments*
Former student re-enactor at Fort George, 2008-2009, a graduate of Broadcasting: Radio, Television and Film program at Niagara College class of 2010 and is currently working for CBC in Toronto as a Broadcast Technician.

THE NIAGARA FRONTIER.

LAKE ONT

Burlington Bay

Cootes Paradise

Big Cr.

Stoney Creek

Burlington

40

30

Dundas

Ancaster

Terriberry

Gees Br

Onondogas